Songs & Scars

Songs & Scars

Bailee Vargas

SONGS AND SCARS

To Mary,
you shall never be forgotten.
Thank you for being there for me.

Table of Contents

The Prayer

When I am empty

fill me.

When there is

nothing left

I will draw from

the wellsprings

of the One

who gave me breath.

Hope

Chapter One

*I pray that your hearts will be flooded
with light so that you can understand
the confident hope He has given
Ephesians 1:18a NLT*

Hope

Show me hope
and I shall embrace it.
The heartbeat of it
breaking through the chaos.
Silencing the noise.
It is something
I can lace my fingers about
and hold steadfast
until the night has passed.
Grasping it as a lantern
light glimmering through glass
reflecting off snowy footsteps.
I ask for hope
as I ask for hearth and home.
It is a foundation
ground I can walk upon
keeping my feet from falling.
Give me hope
and I shall plant it
deep in my heart
not allowing the soil

of my soul

to become desolate.

Strings

The silent strings
designed to hinder the silence
to invade every crevice
until only song is heard.
Vibrating like vocal cords
they invisibly create something.
A sound which ignites
emotion and action.
A song that is without words
and yet communicates.
Meaning that words could
not comprehend.

Wellsprings

There is a place

where there is no such thing as need

where the empty is replaced with overflow.

There is a place

where promises are fulfilled

and life is renewed.

It is the place

where the One who is everything

steps into the in-between

and opens wellsprings.

An everlasting overflow

into these empty crevices.

Change

Life like daydreams
shifting
making a move
across an unsteady
structure called time.
It is a mystery
the changing tides.
Seasons transforming
before we can grasp
the new that
is now
already there.

Home

It is a big, small world.
And yet there is a place
just one; that is yours.
The English language
describes it as home.
It is a miracle of a place,
this place called home.
Some have yet to find it
while others have dug roots deep.
Now home isn't perfect
it's covered in laughter and tears
mud and cake batter.
Yet sometimes, some places
don't have to be perfect
to be good.

Pages

Blank pages

soft whites that open doors.

The very same thing that could be

tossed into the fire, torn into bits.

Can also start something

something deep

something that can surpass time.

For there is something truly powerful

about paper,

a blank slate,

emptiness waiting to be filled.

It is the story of how something

with little to no value

can become something that speaks

to generations

to people after people.

Until blank pages

are no longer blank anymore.

Loved

The aching truth is

that you are loved

and don't even truly

know it yet.

You don't even know

what true love is

and yet that changes nothing

you are loved.

You see,

this love is

not dictated by

your shortcomings.

It's not even

affected by your success.

It is constant

and different.

Different in a way

that all other things

you have called love

don't measure up.

Expectant Heart

These are only partial things

only glimpses of the whole.

These beautiful things

are but shadows

of the more that is to come.

Do not grow weary

expectant heart,

do not cease to wonder

at the life that is

before you

but even more so

at the life that is to come.

The Night

Chapter Two

The day is Yours, also the night;
You established the moon and the sun.
You set all the boundaries of the earth.
Psalm 74:16-17 CSV

The In-Between

That's when you will see it
when the walls cave in
when you can't see
for the darkness has overwhelmed
when all feels lost.
That is where hope will be
the place where peace
surpasses understanding.

Stars

I love the night

but not as one who loves the dark.

Rather I rejoice in the light

that prevails when darkness consumes.

The flickers of hope

dancing across a darkened sky.

Empty

Grasping for rest

we find ourselves

coming back empty handed

from a world where

desolate battles are fought.

Labor without fruit.

Until we find ourselves

seeking a different source

a well that is not empty.

Refusal

I refuse to bow

to a world of change.

An unsteady place

that demands.

An upside down world

we've been made to believe

is right side up.

So that when

good is introduced

it is contrary

to a subjective 'good'

that has been invented.

Until we are accustomed

to a truth that changes.

Truth based

on circumstance.

I refuse

to be tossed about

by a sea of change,

until what I know is real

fades away.

The Cry

What if

we could hear

the cry of creation?

The moaning and

creaking of years.

Distorted figures

fighting to be

put back together

to be made right again.

It is a puzzle that has

for too long been

put out of place.

The Gardener

He is honest

achingly so.

Truth that strips us bare,

leaving us with empty hands.

He is generous

fruitfully so.

Never leaving us with nothing

supplying seeds

where weeds were uprooted.

Look For

I want you to reflect

on days gone by

sunsets, sunrises.

The beautiful, the messy.

The heart-clenching sorrow

the soul resonating joy.

Look for the life

don't miss it.

It dwells in the

every day, the ordinary.

Tucked in between

the consistent ticks of time.

I Miss You

The voice of those who lost a loved one.

I miss you

as I miss the sunlight

once night is upon me.

I miss you with a deep

ache that seeps into my bones.

I miss the time that was only ours

who I was with you.

I hate the hole you left

but love the place you held.

The hollowed out portions of my heart

that you had taken as your own.

I miss you.

My heart beats with the hope of eternity

and yet weeps in the waiting.

Longing for you to be here right now.

I miss you.

Walk with me

Walk with me along this life
as we pave our path
with footsteps side by side.
Hoof prints and paw prints
boots and sandals.
I was not made to walk alone.
Walk with me
create a place by my side
that leaves a hole when
you are no longer there.
Until then we shall
chase each other across
the fields of life
and walk close when
the night gets dark.
We shall fight for one another
in this tug-a-war of death
dancing to the song of life.
Longing for but one
more footstep, side by side.
And when the time comes

and both our roads end

I know I will see you

just as I did back then.

The Morning

Chapter Three

Weeping may last through the night,
but joy comes with the morning.
Psalm 30:5b NLT

Light

The cacophony of rhythm
unrelenting noise that never ceases
drumbeats pounding aimlessly
a disordered melody
high and low fighting for relevance.

And then silence
perfect silence
as if sound no longer existed.
For all that is chaos
has become calm.

The first note started then
hope in its wake.
The cadence of it
echoed off the walls
as more notes joined in song
molding together, becoming one
"Let there be light"

Beyond

I wonder sometimes

where life would take us

if we truly trusted.

If we allowed our souls

to rest upon the

One who made

the ground beneath our feet.

I wonder sometimes

what vastness

lies in a life not held back.

Freedom that defies boundaries.

A flourishing that happens

when the walls are removed.

I wonder sometimes

if limitations are simply illusions,

I wonder sometimes

if we truly know

what the tearing of that veil

meant.

Hot Air Balloons

Fire, warming air.
Its fiery breath colliding
with the summer morning chill.
Loud hot breaths
bouncing off bright colors,
setting the morning aglow.
It is early
that time just before
the songbird sings.
The smell of warm pastries
flooding senses, warming hearts
as bright lights and swirling colors
are lifted into the arena of sky.
Warm air, creating flight
unfurling itself from gravity's hold.
Creating a miracle.
As balloons spread out like
polka dots on quilting fabric
and the sunrise is greeted by
joyous faces.

Movement

Slow and fruitful

like petals unfolding

or vines reaching

for the heavens.

It can also come

with momentum

like the galloping of hooves

movement with purpose

and agility.

There is a power to it

bringing change

breakthrough.

The Dance of Nature

The leaves dance across
a stage of air,
mimicking the design
of fluffy whites gracing
the platform of sky.
Blues and whites mingling
as red, yellow, green
float in the wind.
The song of them
not heard by human ears
and yet they dance.

I Am Thankful

I am thankful for perfection

that cannot be earned or bought.

An image that renews

and restores.

I am thankful for the new

to replace the old.

Life to replace the death.

I am thankful

for the change of seasons

and birdsongs in the morning.

I am thankful for life.

For people and places and things

that take your breath away

that bring perspective.

I am thankful.

I am thankful for you

and the part you play

the color you bring.

I am thankful that you and I

we have breath in our lungs

and blood in our veins.

We have purpose and passion

We have life.

I am thankful.

Perspective

I will readjust my lens

to see that which is

overlooked.

The important details.

The little things

that are in fact

the big things.

I will slow down

and listen

to the music

and voices

that often times

slip through the

cracks of my day.

I will be intentional

with time, with people.

Putting my heart

and soul

into that which

matters

for eternity

Victory

Chapter Four

No, despite all these things,
overwhelming victory is ours through Christ
Romans 8:37a NLT

Victory Song

The song rang out

triumphant over

the wilderness.

Its notes falling softly

down the valley.

It is a beautiful thing:

Victory is

like dew drops falling

on leaves,

on notes,

on strings.

It is a great noise

coming in waves

down a slope of petals,

reclaimed from

the ash it once was, victory.

The Sound

Can't you hear it?

The heart pounding

soul clenching

sound of

light

hitting darkness.

The split second

embrace of

sand and wave.

Green grasping

depth beyond the soil.

Drops of tears

turned blood

turned love soaked

cries

"Why have you forsaken me?"

Do you hear it?

The whisper beyond

the fire

the stone thrown earth

a sound

that breaks through

the boundary

of God and man.

The Gospel

It is a love song,

a living breathing story

made for the ages.

Designed for the ancient

and the new

it transcends time.

The endless cry for renewal,

redemption from failure.

A Creator longing

for a creation

that walked away.

It is marked with

heavy footsteps

of pain and suffering

ultimate sacrifice; love.

It is an endless process

of recreating

that which has been broken.

This is the miracle of our lifetime

the heartbeat of life

overcoming death.

I Ask You

I ask you to be brave

to love deeply and unconditionally.

I ask you to not look back

to give without expecting in return.

I ask you to drink deep

of what life has to offer.

Finding joy hidden in the ordinary.

I ask you to work hard

and always finish what you start.

I ask you to live with humility

and hold every action up with integrity.

I ask you to strive towards holiness

not living for yourself

but for the One who created you.

Known

You were known before you existed.
The purpose and person of you,
already a reality.
Before you had breath
in your lungs and words
on your lips
the One who made you
knew your voice.
He knew the sorrows you'd face
and the burdens you would bear.
You were known
every hair on your head
accounted for.
You were set apart
before the intricate parts of you
were woven in your mother's womb.
You were chosen and loved
before you knew of such things.
You are unique
and designed with vision.
You are known.

Expectant Wonder

I wait for the dawn

an expectancy I have

become accustomed to

and yet fail to see the miracle.

Instead it gets buried beneath

my monotony of days

my shallow thoughts.

When time seems to speed up

not giving time to see things

more than just surface level.

And so, I must force my mind to slow

and command my soul to be still

so I will not miss

the gifts given to me

in between ticks of time.

I will wait with hope filled wonder

for the single second of time

when the light

overcomes the darkness

every single day.

 I will cherish the miracles

found within every little thing.
The small wonders
that bring meaning to a life
of constant movement.
I will be intentional
and filled my days with
an expectancy for wonder
an excitement for what life
has to offer.

Dwell

I will dwell in this peace, this love
that has sought after me.
A God who has asked nothing of me
and yet has given me everything.
The very breath in my lungs, a gift.
My beating heart a testimony of His love.
I will rejoice in the life He has given me
and not lose hope in the purpose
He has laid before me.
I will set my eyes on things above
and not lose sight of that which matters.

New Beginnings

Chapter Five

Therefore, if anyone is in Christ,
he is a new creation; the old has
passed away, and see, the new has come!
2 Corinthians 5:17 CSB

Refining

There is a point when you
have to allow yourself
to be remade.
When it is impossible
to move forward
and remain the same person.
It is the moment when
your breakthrough
is found in your surrender.
When you allow yourself
to once again be placed
on the potter's wheel,
and allow Him to begin
to mold your rough places smooth.
It is an uncomfortable season
this season of change.
And yet it is a requirement
for growth.
A seemingly pointless pain
discomfort, unknowing
that refines us.

Woven

Each strand
colliding with the next
is a perfect pattern.
Over and under
within and around.
Intricately they are placed
allowing what once was
many strands to become
something of unity
a single piece
meticulously woven
from many parts.

We Dream

We dream

of dragons and knights

princesses and happy endings.

Of endless summers

and sandy, salty water beach days.

We dream of adventure

of mountain hikes

and untouched trails.

We dream

our childlike hearts

wanting to fly and float

chasing stars and fireflies.

Satisfying our souls with simple.

We dream.

drinking deep of the

honey of life.

Wondrous wonder.

We dream.

Symphony Sound

The symphony, a sound wave.

Endless ocean waters

crashing into the atmosphere.

The music calmed and swelled

as an ocean tide

the song of ocean shores.

Invading with sound

as great blue depths

captivate the sight.

It is a powerful thing

a beautiful, created thing.

The sound of it,

not soon forgotten

and yet also new.

A song to be discovered.

Creation

It was a silence we could not know

a darkness that could be felt

until noise erupted

and light permeated

a space empty and void

slowly being filled, created.

The sound was deafening

a voice ringing out when

no voice was known.

It brought order to

expanses of confusion.

Bringing something out of

nothing.

A change of days

an establishment of time

as new was created.

A world made to be in

perfect alignment.

Its design a haven for life.

Words and Sounds

Words are meant to tell a story
to create and communicate
to speak to the heart.
They were designed to be
an extension of the soul
an echo of who someone is
drawn out in small squiggles on page.
Music was designed to fill
the quiet, lonesome places
to burrow within the soul
and swirl about the steady
rhythm of the heart.
It is a reflection of the one
behind the instrument.
The one who has set their
hands to creating a sound, a song.

From Old to New

Snowflakes like falling stars

disappearing far too quickly,

glimmers of something

pilling up with abundance

and then trickling away.

Soft greens and sweltering days

like tree leaves

changing, and then falling away.

The wind scattering them

until the crunch of leaves underfoot

becomes fluffy clouds of snow,

which slowly seep into the dry earth

watering roots and seeds

until petals and leaves

are seen once more

beneath a summer sky

of falling stars.

Song of Life

If you listen very closely

you will hear the song.

Sung by life,

it is woven into

the very fabric of this world.

A melody of the ages

from the bird song

to the ocean waves

it is singing.

It is the song found

in the swirl of wind

and the dance

of wooden limbs and leaves.

A noise that

only the soul can hear.

About the Author

With a pen as her paintbrush, Bailee paints meaning with her words. Each line designed to bring hope and life. She is a lover of Jesus, poetry, and stories that reflect truth. Bailee lives on a ranch in Riverton, WY with her family, where she has found a passion for horses and writing.

Let's Connect!

Do you love the words within these pages?

Your review is most welcome anywhere my book is sold.

I would love to hear your thoughts!

For further comments, questions, or fun bookish discussion

visit me on social media

or email me at:

Bailee.v.author@gmail.com

Made in the USA
Middletown, DE
16 January 2023

22252404R00033